A Pocket Guide to

Ha... Lite

You create your own reality.

Jeannette J Sloan

First published in Great Britain in 1998 by
Agape House
16 Simpson Road
Walton Park
Milton Keynes MK7 7HN

A catalogue record for this book is available from the
British Library

ISBN 0 9532105 02

Printed by
Candor Design & Print
Northampton NN3 6AX

DEDICATION

To our beautiful grandchildren Christina, Brittany, Sahara, Zachary and Harry, and to the child within each of us who knows that it's so easy to be happy when we truly enjoy the present moment.

Would you like to join us in enjoying the PRESENT MOMENT a lot more ? If so, this booklet is for you.

PASS IT ON !

The information in this little booklet belongs to the universe - it is simply energy and information flowing through each and everyone of us and cannot be considered the sole property and exclusive right of any one person.

So ... Pass it on - Teach others !   Thank you !!

CONTENTS

DEDICATION

ACKNOWLEDGMENTS

INTRODUCTION

CHAPTER 1   11

Who am I ?
> Understand the process of early programming
> The REAL me or the me I think I am

CHAPTER 2   19

Can I change ?
> Make the decision
> Enough is enough

CHAPTER 3   25

Where do I start ?
> Garbage in, garbage out, positive in, positive out
> Become your own programmer
> Self survey - How wonky is your wheel of life ?
> Who you truly want to be is who you are
> Decide what you want for your life
> Create your new personal blueprint

CHAPTER 4   47

Where do I get the power to change ?
> Present moment motoring
> Tell the TRUTH in advance
> Plant nutritious seeds in the garden of your mind

CHAPTER 5   65

In Conclusion
> A summary

ACKNOWLEDGMENTS

Thank you for taking time to read this booklet. The fact that you have picked it up could mean that you know there is something more to life than what you are experiencing right now - and you would like to know how to access it.

Hopefully you will find a variety of tools and techniques which can help you take greater control of your life NOW, rather than LATER ! What you are about to read may not be new to you, however, it will raise your level of conscious awareness, and in this time-bound existence of ours, if applied, will help you to stop wasting time going around in circles. Take from it what you find helpful and leave aside what you do not. Just remember, we all need to make some changes in our life, and the only time change is painful is when we put up resistance to change or when the change we are facing is not in the direction we want to travel.

The credit for the information within these covers must go to the universal flow of energy and information. The teachers whose wisdom I have assimilated over the past 20 years are numerous. I would like to acknowledge some professional teachers whose lectures, workshops, books and/or audio tapes have helped me to verbalise and formulate this particular course which I have developed particularly for inmates of Woodhill Prison in Milton Keynes, England (I truly believe we are all prisoners of our own intellect and it is our individual responsibility to set ourselves free in order to pioneer our own future): Deepak Chopra, Brian Tracy, Shakti Gawain, Stephen Covey, Tony Quinn, Wayne Dyer, Robert Holden, Louise Hay, Stuart Wilde and Earl Nightingale whose audio tape 'The Strangest Secret' I heard almost 20 years ago, made a profound impact on my life with the simple statement: 'Change your thinking, and you change your life !'.

My very special thanks to my best friend - my husband Don, to our children Stephen, Jacqueline, Jane and Kevin who have been my personal teachers from the moment of their birth and to my 90 year-old father-in-law, Donald Sloan Sr., who continues to inspire me as a living example of what I teach and with his favourite quote: 'You don't stop playing because you grow old, you grow old because you stop playing !'. And thank you, Angie McNabb, for the hours spent helping me to put the words of my course into print - and especially for the creative input of delightful illustrations which you said came directly from the universe. Lots of friends read and proof-read my notes, encouraging and correcting as they were transformed into this final printing - thanks to all of you.

I am eternally grateful for my own discoveries on a daily basis. This IS the greatest time to be alive particularly when we realise that happiness is a journey, not a destination. I wish everyone who reads this booklet a successful journey: travelling with a purpose, travelling light and travelling in good company.

With love and good wishes

Jeannette

INTRODUCTION

An amazing birthright of every human being is the gift of unlimited potential. This evolutionary inheritance is available to us all; but for countless people it remains dormant, or untapped, for their entire lives.

The challenge we face is that we arrive here without a set of instructions ! We don't know what it is we have to do to unlock the treasures of our human legacy.

Every piece of equipment we buy today comes with instructions for use. Yet, men and women, the most complex organisms to evolve on our planet have to figure out how to be happy and successful by trial and error.

Some people seem to have it figured out. They seem to function successfully and happily most of the time quite naturally, while others find life an uphill battle, fraught with setbacks.

What is it that makes the difference ? Are there some simple keys to a happier existence ? Of course, I believe there are - simple, but not easy necessarily ! This printed guide to a happy life covers one area only and rather briefly - how to use your mind to create a more wonderful reality than you are experiencing at this moment in time. I trust it will encourage you to search further.

This brief 'instructional manual' comes to you with love and a profound desire to share with you some of the insights that have helped me and countless others to achieve greater personal fulfilment in our day to day living. I trust you will enjoy this straight-forward explanation of why you are the way you are and some simple things you can do to access the boundless opportunities for better health, wealth and happiness that lie within you - no matter where you are right now.

WHO AM I ?

ENTER, NEW LIFE ...

You came into this world as pure potential ...
totally positive - trusting - loving

Even though your childhood

is **very** important,

it is not so much

WHAT

happens

to you ...

but rather

what **YOU MAKE** of

what happens

to you ...

that really counts !

LET'S START AT THE VERY BEGINNING !

A new human arrives with a clean slate.

Your natural state is love, trust, wholeness.

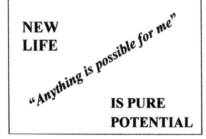

NEW LIFE *"Anything is possible for me"* **IS PURE POTENTIAL**

As a baby you are totally open to all influences - POSITIVE OR NEGATIVE

BABIES ARE NOT BORN NEGATIVE.

(have you ever seen a negative baby ?)

IT'S A VERY GOOD PLACE TO START !

From the moment you were born, you were inundated with **'thought programmes'** from parents, siblings, relatives etc. Your unsuspecting, receptive self, **absorbed** external opinions and information.

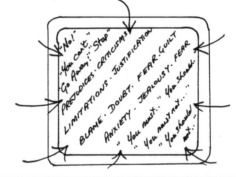

BY THE AGE OF 5 OR 6
YOU WERE ALREADY WEARING
A CLOAK OF CONDITIONING.

Research tells us the input ratio of **negative** to **positive**
is

8 : 1

(making conditioning in our society very negative indeed)

REMEMBER - ALL NEGATIVITY IS **LEARNED**

MUSIC FADES
(as we reach the 'C' FACTOR !)

By the age of 18 the **'negative input'**
has solidified into your personality or **EGO** !

AND YOU BELIEVE THIS IS **PERMANENT** !

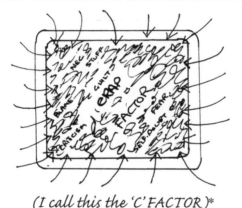

(I call this the 'C' FACTOR)*

RESULT ?

The anti-life build up makes you no more
than a robot
where you feel you have
little or no control in your life
and
where change seems IMPOSSIBLE ! **BUT...**

*'C' meaning negative **CONDITIONING** or **CRAP** !

16

THE WONDERFUL TRUTH IS...

The REAL YOU - full of love, hope,
compassion etc., is still there

underneath the pile of negativity is

YOUR TRUE MAGNIFICENT SELF !

You **CAN**

REDISCOVER your

FANTASTIC HUMAN LEGACY
OF
PURE POTENTIAL

CAN I CHANGE ?

WHAT DO YOU THINK ?

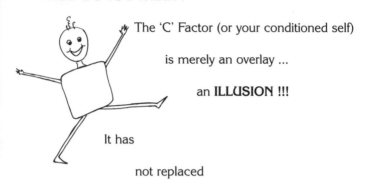

The 'C' Factor (or your conditioned self)

is merely an overlay ...

an **ILLUSION !!!**

It has

not replaced

the

REAL YOU !

(you really are there, full of all the original potential)

Lifelong bombardment
of negativity

simply forms a MASK !

'I CAN CHOOSE TO CHANGE'

'I CAN DISCARD MY MASK OF PAST
CONDITIONING'

THE MAGICAL TRUTH IS...

YOU REALLY DO HAVE

FATHOMLESS DEPTHS

... JUST WAITING TO BE PLUMBED !

Admit to yourself that deep down you quietly know you
are a capable and worthwhile person.

*(Most of us **can feel** this truth
at a very private 'gut' level).*

EXTERNAL NEGATIVES CREATED A

DOWNWARD SPIRAL

PROPELLING US

UNCONSCIOUSLY TO LIVING

UNDER A CLOUD

'IN THE LAND OF FEAR'

MAKE THE **DECISION** TO CHANGE ------
(now that you know you can !)

CLARITY OF PURPOSE

QUIET CONFIDENCE AND

BUILDING SELF ESTEEM

AN UPWARD SPIRAL

INTERNAL POSITIVES CREATE

LIVING 'IN THE LAND OF LOVE' -

firstly by loving yourself

(come with me ... I'll show you how ...

IT'S SIMPLE
but it's not easy!

A

Build up of stuff over twenty, thirty, forty or even fifty years plus, results in feelings of self-doubt, worry, guilt, insecurity, fear, envy, self-pity... in short...

A LACK OF SELF-ESTEEM.

B

Because your negativity is **learned** - when you choose to take control of your life you can **DETACH** from the 'C' FACTOR build-up and move on....

D

awaiting blue-print

C *Plop!*

... to fulfil your limitless potential as you go on with the rest of your life.

WHERE DO I START ?

LET'S USE THE ANALOGY OF A COMPUTER

(since we live in a technological world)

If you see your mind

    as the **HARDWARE**

And all the conditioning (programming)
over the years

    as the **SOFTWARE**

    (garbage in, garbage out
       positive in, positive out)...

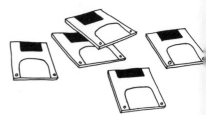

THEN ...

    WHO IS ...

        THE PROGRAMMER ?

Over the years you have chosen to believe all the labels, negativity etc. that have been thrown at you (even if you don't know it) and, in effect, until now ...

YOU CHOSE TO CONTINUE THE PAST PROGRAMMING.

(by keeping this belief system alive)

THE CHOICE NOW IS

     a) to continue thinking, speaking and acting in the same old way *(the easy route)*

or   b) to change the programming - the SOFTWARE *(challenging but worth the effort)*

THIS MEANS **ACTIVELY SEEKING** MORE POSITIVE,

UPLIFTING, LIFE ENHANCING INFORMATION

HELPING YOU TO GET YOUR LIFE

IN BALANCE !

'I AM RESPONSIBLE FOR MY LIFE !'

'I CHOOSE TO BECOME THE BEST
PERSON I CAN BE'

'I AM A VALUABLE AND WORTHWHILE
PERSON'

'I CAN MAKE A DIFFERENCE'

THE SELF SURVEY !

THINK ABOUT WHO YOU ARE TODAY ...

ASK YOURSELF:

'Do I enjoy life ?'
'How contented am I ?'
'Am I as healthy as I'd like to be ?'
'Do I enjoy good relationships.....
.....at home ? .....at work ?.....socially ?'
'Do I feel secure ? Financially ? Emotionally ?'
'Does my life have purpose ? Goals ? Dreams ?'
'Do I really like myself ?' Are there things
I'd like to change in my life ?' 'How
well do I really know myself ?'
'Am I confident ?' 'Do I
believe in myself ?'
'Is there room
for

i

m

p

r

o

v

e

m

e

n

t

?'

THE WHEEL OF LIFE ...
and what it says to you !

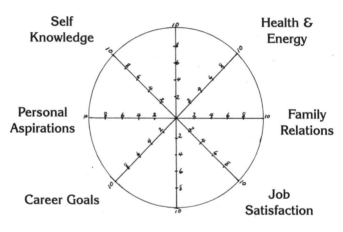

Each spoke of the wheel represents a different facet of life
Add/delete any that are/are not specific to you.

Give yourself a rating between 1 and 10 (10 being excellent) to express your feeling of fulfilment in each of these 8 key areas of life.

Mark an X on each spoke to illustrate your chosen rating.

(some people have been known to mark a minus 2 occasionally !)

REMEMBER - Self-honesty is the start of any real change.

TURN TO THE NEXT PAGE **ONLY** WHEN YOU HAVE COMPLETED THIS EXERCISE.

HOW WONKY IS YOUR WHEEL ?

To find out, turn back to the previous page and join your
8 X's with straight lines. This exercise may reveal how
well balanced your life is at present.

(In our example on this page,
the wonky wheel demonstrates
IMBALANCE !)

**Peace &
Contentment**

**Self
Knowledge**

**Health &
Energy**

**Personal
Aspirations**

**Family
Relations**

Career Goals

**Job
Satisfaction**

Financial Security

Definition of 'wonky': 1.unsteady, 2.askew,
3.liable to break down

REMEMBER: Your assessment in each of the 8 key
areas of life is

HOW YOU FEEL **TODAY** !

(this can change from day to day)

BALANCE IS ESSENTIAL TO HAPPINESS

Most of your problems occur
when you are out of balance, right ?

THIS GRAPHIC VIEW OF YOUR LIFE
INDICATES THE TROUBLE SPOTS TO FOCUS ON.

DECIDE WHAT TO FOCUS ON

Write down the areas from your "wheel" that
you'd most like to focus on:

_____

_____

_____

_____

_____

What would you truly like to accomplish by working
through this little book ?

_____

_____

_____

_____

IDENTIFY YOUR

STRENGTHS (that enhance your life)	**"GIFTS"** (that are your teachers)
Enthusiasm	Apathy
Courage	Fear
Self-confidence	Self-doubt
Responsibility	Blame
Persistence	Procrastination
Patience	Exasperation
Honesty	Dishonesty
Compassion	Resentment
Joy	Despair
Discipline	Lack of discipline
Calmness	Agitation
Passion	Indifference
Kindness	Bitterness
Flexibility	Fixed ideas
Tolerance	Prejudice
Good sense of humour	Taking things too seriously
_____	_____
_____	_____
_____	_____
_____	_____

Place an asterisk beside the 2 or 3 main qualities you would like to **ENHANCE**, and the 2 or 3 characteristics you would like to **LEARN FROM** and possibly **ELIMINATE**. Add any of importance to you.

WHO IS

RESPONSIBLE

FOR BRINGING ABOUT

THE **CHANGES**

YOU WANT IN

YOUR LIFE ?

YOU !

(If you want to continue making excuses, stop reading and go back to page 13 !)

NOW YOU ARE READY

TO CREATE YOUR

PERSONAL BLUEPRINT

If there was nothing holding you back ...

HOW WOULD YOU LIVE YOUR LIFE ?

* What lifestyle would you choose ?

 * How much energy would you have ?

  * What sort of relationships would you have ?

   * What sort of lover would you be ?

    * What financial objectives would you set ?

     * What courses / seminars would you attend ?

      * What new subject would you like to learn about ?

       * What kind of father / mother would you like to be ?

        * How would you want to feel about yourself ?

CLARITY IS POWER !

CONSIDER EACH OF THE 8 KEY AREAS

How would it feel to be living a 10/10 life ?

_____

_____

_____

_____

YOUR CHOICE !

Describe your ideal day, in detail:

_____

_____

_____

_____

_____

_____

_____

_____

Describe the qualities of your ideal relationship:

_____

_____

_____

_____

Describe the qualities of your ideal job / career / hobby:

_____

_____

_____

_____

Describe in a positive way any other area of your life that you would like to experience differently:

_____

_____

_____

_____

BLOCKAGES - that drag you down

It can be helpful to recognise the SHADOW SIDE of yourself - especially if you want to change - BUT, do you have to keep bombarding yourself ?

(it is estimated that we think 60,000 thoughts per day --- can you guess what the great majority of them are like ?)

'I'm never on time.' 'That's just the way I am.'

'I'm so stupid. How could I do such a thing.'

'I'll never make enough money to pay my bills.'

'I'll be happy if...and when...'

'I'm not good enough.'

'Poor me, I've had a rough time lately.'

'Nobody cares anyway, why should I ?'

'I can't help getting angry when everything goes wrong.'

Etc. etc. etc. ...

DO YOU WANT TO REMAIN A 'VICTIM' **ALL** YOUR LIFE ?

IF NOT IT'S SIMPLE .....

CHANGE !

Change what you say !

ESPECIALLY

What you say:

TO YOURSELF

ABOUT YOURSELF !

YOU BECOME WHAT YOU THINK ABOUT !

THE "ME" I WANT TO BE

It's time to "BE" the person you KNOW YOU CAN BE:

It's time to start sowing some positive seeds.

WHAT IS THE REALITY YOU WANT ?

Do you want to remain the same person ? If so, keep doing and saying exactly what you're doing and saying - that ENSURES you will never change.

OR

Do you want to be your TRUE MAGNIFICENT SELF ??? If so, you need to apply some effort into changing what you think, say and do.

DESCRIBE YOURSELF AS YOU KNOW YOU ARE (deep down): if this is difficult - think of a good wise person who has your best interests at heart and who loves you very much - what would he/she say about who you are ?

_____

_____

_____

_____

_____

_____

Very few people will do this kind of exercise **BECAUSE...**

it just takes too much effort !!

EVERYONE IS CARRYING A HEAVY LOAD !

(Our parents and children are,
our friends and associates are...
*...we are **all** burdened by life's 'C' FACTOR, right ?)*

GET SMART - DUMP IT !

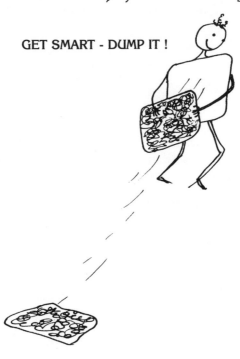

it is **YOUR CHOICE** !

WHERE DO I GET THE POWER TO CHANGE ?

THINK !

WHERE IS

THE POWER

TO CHANGE ?

Most people consider their life by looking **backward** at where they've come from, which is like standing on a ship's stern...

... observing the wake!

DOES THE WAKE POWER THE SHIP ?

NO!

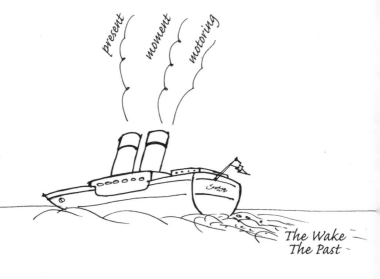

The Wake —
The Past -

**The ship is powered by
PRESENT MOMENT MOTORING
responding to commands from the captain.**

CAPTAIN YOUR OWN SHIP !

DECIDE WHERE YOU WANT TO GO !

GIVE YOURSELF NEW COMMANDS!

YOUR

POINT OF POWER

IS IN THE

PRESENT MOMENT !

WHEN YOU TALK TO YOURSELF !

Your **subconscious** mind is always listening
and works best
on instructions from you -
and most effectively when those instructions
are delivered by your **conscious** mind
in a very specific way

It's important to give yourself specific instructions

- ## In the first <u>P</u>erson
- ## <u>P</u>ositively
- ## In the <u>P</u>resent tense

i.e.   'I feel terrific !'
'I like myself !'
'I am responsible for my life !'
'I am a very patient mother/father !'
'I refuse to procrastinate on any task !'
'I enjoy being debt free !'

Create your own PPP statements...

It may feel like a

BIG LIE !

BUT ...if what you express in this way is in line with

your **VALUES**

and your chosen **PERSONAL BLUEPRINT**

It can become the

BIG TRUTH !

in your life !

Talk to yourself as though what you want **has already taken place**.

This is called ...TELLING THE TRUTH **IN ADVANCE !**

*(the thoughts you are thinking
and the words you are speaking TODAY,
are truly creating your future)*

CHOOSE AND USE GOOD POSITIVE PROGRAMMING !

Here are some self talk statements you can use to help you get started:

- 'I am creative and receive all the ideas I need to reach my goals'

- 'I am well organised and have everything in it's place'

- 'I feel healthy and full of energy'

- 'I keep my life in balance each day'

- 'I enjoy having a positive bank balance and being able to meet all expenses with effortless ease'

- 'I am eager and willing to be my true magnificent self'

- 'I am excellent at my chosen career and I am proud of the work I do'

- 'I eat wholesome and well balanced meals'

HERE'S THE PROCESS ...

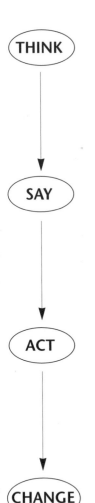

THINK

Listen to your mental chatter.
Catch yourself saying negative things to yourself and others and shout '**STOP**' !

Ask yourself - 'Is this the life I want ?'
'Is this the person I want to be ?'
No ! So, substitute your PPP statements
Keep your thoughts on what you want
not on what you don't want !!!

SAY

Only speak in positive terms -
'I am a loving, gentle person'
'I refuse to blame anyone, anymore'
'I am responsible for my actions'
Begin speaking the statements from your new
PERSONAL BLUEPRINT

ACT

TODAY - **NOW** ! - 'Act as if...'
Start to behave as though you already are the person you'd like to be.
ACT OUT the characteristics you've announced in your PPP statements or in your
PERSONAL BLUEPRINT !

Work at this on a regular basis and change will occur as surely as night follows day !

CHANGE

(It won't happen all at once -
Don't worry if you fall back into old ways -
Pick yourself up and repeat the process).

WRITE YOUR OWN SELF TALK STATEMENTS

OR **AFFIRMATIONS**

TO HELP YOU BRING ABOUT THE CHANGES

YOU HAVE EXPRESSED IN YOUR

PERSONAL BLUEPRINT

_____
_____
_____
_____
_____
_____
_____
_____
_____
_____
_____
_____

Every morning wake up and say:

"I CHOOSE TO HAVE A GREAT DAY ...

NO MATTER WHAT"

"I BELIEVE SOMETHING WONDERFUL IS GOING TO

HAPPEN TO ME TODAY"

"I FEEL TERRIFIC !"

*(prepare to be surprised at
the difference this will make !)*

IT'S SO SIMPLE
that's probably why we've missed it!

a   Affirmations are much more effective when said aloud or written down - start by writing three or four, and build up to ten or twelve.

'I enjoy taking control of my life!'

b   Repetition is important - every single day -several times a day. Remember that your existing belief system has taken twenty, thirty, forty or even fifty plus years to develop.

'I feel healthy; I feel good; I feel prosperous!'

c   Write each affirmation at least three times each. It is helpful to buy a small exercise book for this purpose. Use a page a day - amazing changes will occur in your life before this book is filled.

'I am a very confident and well organised person'

d   Your mind always moves you toward what you think about.

'I keep my thoughts on what I want to happen'

e   Keep this confidential as you work on yourself - soon enough your friends and associates will notice the change in you.

'I am a worthwhile and valuable person'

'I make a difference'

JUST WHEN YOU THINK
YOU'VE GOT THE MESSAGE

I'M HERE TO REMIND YOU ...

EVERYTHING COUNTS !

Self-instruction is the most important ingredient
for change
BUT
what you tell yourself is not
the only input received by your mind.

IF YOU ARE **REALLY SERIOUS** ABOUT YOUR FUTURE,

YOU MUST BECOME CONSCIOUS

OF

ALL INCOMING DATA

BECOME SELECTIVE !

Surround yourself with: POSITIVE books

POSITIVE people

and   POSITIVE INFORMATION

(magazines, newspapers, courses, tapes etc...)

Be prepared to let go of negative situations and negative people as you make the changes (neg. friends, neg. work environment, neg. newspapers etc.).

INCREASE YOUR EXPOSURE TO THOSE THINGS
THAT ARE IN LINE WITH

YOUR HIGHEST VALUES...

AND WITH YOUR NEW PERSONAL BLUEPRINT
(the you, you want to be)

● WATCH WHAT YOU WATCH ! (TV, VIDEO, FILMS etc.)

● THERE ARE **NO EXCEPTIONS** -----

EVERYTHING HAS AN EFFECT

'IF IT'S TO BE, IT'S UP TO ME !'

AS YE SOW

SO SHALL YE REAP

*(what will your garden look like next month,
next year ?)*

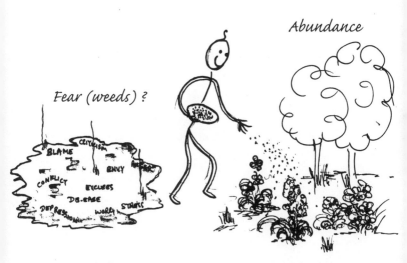

Abundance

Fear (weeds) ?

PLANT NOTHING

PLANT SMALL SEEDS

IT CAN BE FUN TO

START AGAIN WITH

NOURISHING, POSITIVE 'THOUGHT SEEDS':

'I choose to make today the most wonderful day by
thinking only positive thoughts'.

'I sow positive, loving, nutritious seeds in the garden
of my mind'

'I am responsible for the quality of my emotional life !'

'I am responsible for the quality of my financial life !'

'I am responsible for the quality of my physical life !'

'I am responsible for the quality of my mental life !'

'I am responsible for the quality of my spiritual life !'

'IF IT'S TO BE...

IT'S UP TO

YOU !'

IN CONCLUSION

SUMMARY:

- You now understand you were born as **pure potential**

  Nobody is born a 'drop-out', a 'rat-bag', a tinker, tailor, soldier...rich man...poor man...thief...

- You still **are** pure potential

  The concept you have had of yourself in the past has been developed over the years through 'programming'

  Under the pile of negativity is your true magnificent self.

- **You** are now the programmer of your own life

  You decide whether to let yourself down or build yourself up

  'If it's to be, it's up to me !'

- It takes a conscious **DECISION** to leave your negative traits, beliefs, experiences, etc. by the side of the road and **get on** with the rest of your life.

NOW COMES THE EFFORT

• Decide to create a new PERSONAL BLUEPRINT

• Check your starting point:

   Who do I think I am now ?
   Who is the "ME" I want to be ?

• Create 10 - 12 positive affirmations

   This is - 'TELLING THE TRUTH IN ADVANCE'
   Think, say and act as if you already are
   that person

   (you really are that person, let him/her out !!)

YOUR

POINT OF POWER

IS IN

THE PRESENT MOMENT

- **FEED YOUR MIND** - every single day

      positive thoughts
      positive books, tapes, courses
      positive people
      positive TV, films, newspapers

- **EVERYTHING COUNTS**

Remember -

Your THOUGHTS are the only thing

in the world that you

can control.

CHOOSE WISELY

TO REALLY MAKE IT WORK

● **Develop an ATTITUDE of GRATITUDE**

Be grateful for all the wonderful little things that happen each day - make a list

Look for the good in everyone and every event

● **Be DETERMINED**

Continually plant nutritious, positive seeds

Keep your mind on what you want in your life

● **Be PERSISTENT**

Persistence is the measure of your belief in yourself

NEVER...NEVER...NEVER GIVE UP !

The **PAST** is history,

The **FUTURE** is a mystery,

The **PRESENT MOMENT** ...

is a **GIFT**.

That's why it's called ...

'THE PRESENT' !

And the gift is **YOURS** for the taking.

If you find some of this material helpful:

PASS IT ON !

TEACH OTHERS !

If you would like to take part in a workshop to study and/or discuss this further:

Or if you would like to purchase extra copies to pass on to friends and associates:

Or if you are interested in A Pocket Guide to A HAPPY LIFE - Book 2:

CALL OR WRITE TO:

AGAPE HOUSE
16 Simpson Road
Walton Park
Milton Keynes MK7 7HN
England

Tel: 01908-201113 Fax: 01908-392203
e-mail: djsloan@compuserve.com